MY TWO COUNTRIES

BY
LADY NANCY ASTOR

Published by Left of Brain Books

Copyright © 2021 Left of Brain Books

ISBN 978-1-396-31922-8

First Edition

Table of Contents

AMERICA

I[1]

"I can conceive of nothing worse than a man-governed world—
except a woman governed world."

I KNOW that this welcome has nothing to do with me. Ever since I first entered the Mother of Parliaments I realised that I had ceased to be a person and had become a symbol. The safe thing about being a symbol is this—you realise that you of yourself can do nothing, but what you symbolise gives you courage and strength, and should give you wisdom. I certainly have been given courage and strength. I won't say too much about wisdom.

My entrance into the House of Commons was not, as some thought, in the nature of a revolution. It was simply evolution. It is interesting how it came about. My husband was the one who started me off on this downward career—from home to the House. If I have helped the cause of women, he is the one to thank—not me. He is a strange and remarkable man. First, it was strange to urge his wife to take up public life, especially as he is a most domesticated creature; but the truth is, he is a born social reformer. He has avoided the pitfalls which so many well-to-do men fall into. He doesn't think that you can right wrongs with philanthropy. He realises that you must go to the bottom of the causes of wrongs and not simply gild over the top. For eleven years I had helped him with his work at Plymouth. Mine was the personal side. I found out the wrongs and he tried to right them. It was a wonderful and happy combination, and I often wish that it was still going on. However, I am not here to tell you of his work, but it is interesting in so far as it shows you how it came about that I stood for Parliament at all. Unless he had been the kind of man that he was, I don't believe that the first woman Member of the oldest Parliament in the world would have come from Plymouth—and that would have been a pity.

---

[1] Before the League of Women Voters, New York.

Plymouth is an ideal port to sail from or to. It has bidden "God Speed" to so many voyagers. I felt that I was embarking on a voyage of faith, but when I arrived at my destination some of the Honourable Members looked upon me more as a pirate than a Pilgrim! A woman in the House of Commons! It was almost enough to have broken up the House. I don't blame them, but it was as hard on the woman as it was on them. Pioneers may be picturesque figures, but they are often rather lonely ones. I must say though, for the House of Commons, they bore their shock with dauntless decency. No body of men could have been kinder and fairer than they were. When you hear people over here trying to run down England, please remember that England first gave the vote to women, and that the men of England welcomed an American-born woman in the House with a fairness and justice which this woman, at least, will never forget.

Different Members received me in different ways. I shall never forget a Scottish Labour man coming up to me, after I had been in the House a little time, and telling me that I wasn't a bit the sort of woman he thought I was going to be; and on being pressed as to what kind of woman he thought I would be, said, "I'll not tell you that, but I know now that you are an ordinary, homely kind of woman"; and he has proved it since by often asking my advice on domestic questions. Then the Irishman—an Irish Member once said to me, "I don't know what you are going to speak about, but I am here to back you." The last was a regular old Noah's Ark man, a typical English Squire type. After two years and a half of never agreeing on any point with me, he remarked to someone that I was a very stupid woman, but he must add, a very attractive one, and he feared I was a thoroughly honest social reformer. I might add that, being the first woman, I had to take up many causes which no one would call exactly popular. I also had to go against the prejudice of generations, but I must say their courtesy has never failed, though my Parliamentary manners must have been somewhat of a trial.

Now I must leave the more personal side and get to what it is all about, and why we are here.

Some women have always been in politics, and not done badly either. It was when we had the Lancastrian kings that it was said that kings were made by Act of Parliament—they ruled by means of Parliament. Then Henry VIII accepted the principle of the Lancastrians to rule by Parliament, but he used that principle in an entirely different way. He made Parliament the engine of his will, he pressed or frightened it into doing anything he wished. Under his guidance Parliament defied and crushed all other powers spiritual and temporal, and he did things which no king or Parliament had ever attempted to do, things unheard of and terrible. Then Elizabeth came along. It is true she scolded her Parliaments for meddling with matters with which, in her opinion, they had no concern, and more than once soundly rated the Speaker of the Commons, but she never carried her quarrels too far, and was able to end her disputes by clever compromise; in other words, she never let Parliament down, and that is what I don't believe any wise woman will do, in spite of the fears of some of the men.

Now why are we in politics? What is it all about? Something much bigger than ourselves. Schopenhauer was wrong in nearly everything he wrote about women—and he wrote a lot—but he was right in one thing. He said, in speaking of women, "The race is to her more than the individual," and I believe that it is true. I feel somehow we do care about the race as a whole; our very natures makes us take a forward vision. There is no reason why women should look back. Mercifully, we have no political past; we have all the mistakes of one-sex legislation, with its appalling failures, to guide us. We should know what to avoid. It is no use blaming the men—we made them what they are—and now it is up to us to try and make ourselves—the makers of men—a little more responsible. We realise that no one sex can govern alone I believe that one of the reasons why civilisation has failed so lamentably is that it has had one sided government. Don't let us make the mistake of ever allowing that to happen again. I can conceive of nothing worse than a man-governed world except a woman-governed world—but I can see the combination of the two going forward, and making civilisation, more worthy of the name of civilisation based on Christianity, not on force—a civilisation based on justice and mercy. I feel men have a greater sense of justice, and we of mercy. They must borrow our mercy and we must use their justice.

We are new brooms. Let us see that we sweep the right rooms. Personally, I feel that every woman should take an active part in local government. I don't mean by that, that every woman should go in for a political career—that, of course, would be absurd; but you can take an active part in local government without going in for a political career. You can be certain when casting your vote that you are casting it for what seems nearest right—for what seems more likely to help the majority and not to bolster up an organised minority. There is a lot to be done in local politics, and it is a fine apprenticeship for central government; it is very practical, but I think that, although practical, it is too near to be attractive.

The things that are far away are more apt to catch our imagination than the ones which are just under our noses, and then, they are often less disagreeable.

Political development is like all other development. We must begin with ourselves, our own consciousness, and clean out our own hearts before we take on the job of putting others straight. So with politics. If we women put our hands to local politics, we must begin with the foundations. After all, central governments only echo local ones; the politician in Washington, if he is a wise man, will always have one eye on his constituency. Let us make that constituency so clean, so straight, so high in its purpose, that the man from home will not dare to take a small, limited view about any question, be it a national or an international one. You must remember that what women are up against is not what they see, but the unseen forces. We are up against generations and generations of prejudice. Ever since Eve ate the apple—but I would like to remind you, and all men, why she ate the apple. It was not simply because it was good for food or pleasant to the eyes: it was from a tree whose fruit would make one wise—"She took of the fruit thereof and did eat, and gave unto her husband with her and he did eat." We have no record of Adam murmuring against the fruit—of his doing anything but eat it with docility. In passing, also, I would like to say that the first time Adam had a chance he laid the blame on woman—however, we will leave Adam.

Ever since woman's consciousness has looked beyond the material, man's consciousness has feared her vaguely; he has gone to her for inspiration, he has relied on her for all that is best and most ideal in his life, yet by sheer material force he has limited her. The Western man has, without knowing it, Westernised the harem mind of the East. I don't believe he knows it yet, so we must break it to him gently. We must go on being his guide, his mother, and his better half. But we must prove to him that we are a necessary half, not only in private, but in political life. The best way that we can do that is to show him that our ambitions are not personal. Let men see that we desire a better, safer, and cleaner world for our children and their children, and that we believe that it is only by doing our bit, by facing unclean things with cleanliness, by facing wrongs with right, by going fearlessly into all things that may be disagreeable, that we will, somehow, make this a little better world. I don't know that we are going to do this—I don't say that women will change the world, but I do say that they can if they want to. Coming, as I do, from the Old World which has seen a devastating war, I cannot face the future without this hope—that the women of all countries will do their duty and raise a generation of men and women who will look upon war and all that leads to it with as much horror as we now look upon a cold-blooded murder. If we want this new world, we can get it only by striving for it; and the real struggle will be within ourselves, to put out of our hearts and of our thoughts, all that makes for war, hate, envy, greed, pride, force, and material ambition.

II[2]

*"I seem a symbol—a sort of connecting link between
the English-speaking people!"*

I AM not really afraid to speak here to-night. I was a little afraid last night—I didn't know quite whether New York audiences would be as kind as Plymouth audiences. I see that they are much the same. They forgive any shortcomings in the way of scholarly attainments or oratorical orations when they see that you are speaking from your heart. I usually do speak from my heart. It has been a safer guide to me than my head, and here to-night it's easy; for surely no people on earth have understood a woman's heart better than the English speaking nations.

Last night I told the Women Voters that I was not a person, but a symbol; to-night I still seem a symbol—a sort of connecting link between the English-speaking people, a frail link, perhaps, but a link that is stronger than it looks. It is a strange thing that England's first woman Member of Parliament should have come from England's first colony. I doubt if the first English woman to land in Virginia was less expected on these shores, than the first Virginian woman to land in the House of Commons was expected on that floor. However, in spite of having neither beads nor fire water, the natives were amazingly kind to that Virginian settler. It is all very picturesque when one thinks of it historically, but it seems very ordinary when it is done. History, I think, is more romantic to read than to make, and I apologise now to future little schoolgirls for having added another question to the endless ones which still haunt me when my mind turns back to the long list of historical personages, varying from Lucretia Borgia down to Susan B. Anthony.

I have been asked what my visit here was for. Cannot a person come home without being suspected of deep and ulterior motives? I may tell you at once, I am not on a mission to promote a better understanding between England and America. No person, however keen about it, can do much in that line. Things which are worth while are made by something better than missions or

---

treaties. They are made only by great ideals in the hearts of the common people.

I don't believe that trade agreements will succeed in promoting a better understanding. But I do say that if the greatest commonwealth of nations the world has ever seen and the greatest federation of states the world has ever known cannot be brought together by some common cause, some human hope and purpose, then I, personally, should feel like the Queen of Sheba—the spirit would go out of me. I do believe that these two nations are bound together by a common cause; and that cause, one of human hope and purpose, is peace on earth and good-will toward all men.

The Washington Conference was not a surprise to me. I knew that England was not a militarist nation any more than America was, and I knew, too, that once they talked things over they would see the utter futility of building battleships against one another. America and England should have the largest fleets because they will certainly use them more as policemen than as fighting forces. After all, when England had the greatest navy in the world she never used it except to keep the freedom of the seas. I often wonder whether Imperialist Germany might not have treated the Monroe Doctrine like a scrap of paper had her fleet been the strongest in the world. However, I don't want to go back to an ancient grudge. It's hopeless trying to go forward when you are looking backward. It is a great mistake to keep such things alive; it only means trouble, and surely there is enough trouble in the world now without looking backward.

America, I am told, draws back with horror when she looks at Europe. I don't blame her. Certainly, it is a sad enough sight to make one drawback. I cannot believe, though, that standing back is the right way to help, and I don't believe that any part of the world can go forward in the truest sense while another part is suffering desperately. The war has shown us that the world is really round and is part interdependent. I am struck more and more by the way in which our stock of moral good-will on both sides is still thwarted by the extent of our misunderstanding.

This not only hinders the recovery of hundreds of millions of people from all the mischiefs of war, but works new mischief of its own. I am thinking now, not so much of America and Britain, who have had their heart-to-heart explanations at the Washington Conference, with an effect which ought to make their relations foolproof, in spite of the small people who are so blinded by their fear or envy and hate, that they would do all in their power to pull them apart. But I am not afraid of them. I am only sorry for them. There is nothing more pitiful than people who are moved by envy or hate, and there is nothing weaker than people who fear. Envy and hate are the most blinding things on earth; it is only people with vision who never perish. When I talk of misunderstanding I am thinking of Europe.

I know that both America and England feel that Europe is not getting on with the peace, that she still has large armies, still fights, and at the same time cries out for help. Russia and France still have great armies, and this naturally makes smaller states arm too. Of course it is all desperately disappointing to some of us. We had hoped that this was a war to end wars—I think it has ended the biggest wars, yet there seem to be a few small private wars going on, and still a great deal of fear and hatred left. I am sure that you will never end war with wars.

I believe that the safest and surest way to get out of war is to join some sort of league of nations. That misrepresented and much despised League has already prevented three small wars, it has registered over one hundred treaties, has repatriated nearly four hundred thousand prisoners—not a bad record for only half a league. I think it is enough to make every woman in America want to join it in some form or other, certainly any of those who have had sons in the war. It is the memory of the anguish of the mothers and fathers who watched for four years which gives me the courage to speak plainly here to-night. You see, the anguish in a mother's heart is felt in all other mothers' hearts over the world, even though they be enemy mothers. If this is true, mothers in any country can be members. I was told to be careful. Why careful? Of what? I have not anything to say that could hurt any one in America, and I only want to try and help the thousands of people in less fortunate countries than America. Anyhow, I do believe that America likes people to say what they mean and care about.

No one could say that America does not care about Europe. Look at the way the American Relief Committee is helping Russia. It is the admiration of the whole of England; often I have heard it referred to in the House of Commons. Yet I don't believe that the greatest philanthropy in the world can add much to the permanent reconstruction of the world, and that is what the world needs more now than anything—reconstruction. It is all very well to hear people talk of European entanglements, but the world is already tangled, and we have to think of a plan to disentangle ourselves. No one could think that English fathers and mothers—with nearly eight hundred thousand sons who will never return—would want to join in a League which would entangle them or any one else in war. The English know enough about wars never to want to fight or to see any one else have to fight. These mothers and fathers think, as I feel sure the fathers and mothers of America do, that the safest and sanest way to get out of wars is to join some sort of association of nations for peace. The Washington Conference shows us what can happen when great countries with great ideals get together. The difference between people with ideals and people without is simply the difference between Pagans and Christians—a Pagan is a man whose standard of right does not extend beyond his own interest Now we Anglo-Saxons rather pride ourselves that our civilisation was built on Christianity. If that is the case, there is no doubt that a lot of Pagans have slipped in among us—perhaps they have also been proselytising. Don't let us proselytise too far, don't let us forget the faith of our forefathers. It must have taken a tremendons faith mixed with a double dose of courage to have crossed the Atlantic in a shell of a boat—yet they did. They were not Pagans. Civilisation has been nearly destroyed by Pagans. We cannot give them a second chance. It is wonderfully helpful to look back and see the kind of men in all countries who have made civilisation. They were not men who carried a grudge, they were not men who hated, but men with an inner consciousness of what man really is capable of, men who realised that life is redeemed only by a purpose bigger than themselves, and a love which passes all understanding.

III[3]

"We must put into public life those qualities which women have had to put into their home life."

IT seems a strange thing to be here—but my life is a little like that of Alice in Wonderland. It gets curiouser and curiouser. When I sailed from Plymouth to the House of Commons, I may tell you frankly I didn't half realise what the voyage would be like. I soon discovered that it was the kind of voyage which would take the spiritual faith of the Pilgrim Fathers and the courage of Sir Francis Drake. They both sailed from my port, and I have had to use both their courage and their faith.

However, I think women possess both courage and faith. When I speak of women I don't mean every woman, I mean real women, women who care about real things—the sort of women who have not only borne men, but have given them such unselfish love that the world has seen, through them, a bit of what the love of God is like.

Now, if we possess courage and faith, it will be no use to us unless we use it. Faith is like a belief—it is only helpful if it leads us to knowledge. Belief in God will only help us if it leads us to knowledge of God.

So we women must turn to account some of this courage and faith. We must put into public life these qualities which women have had to and which they have rejoiced to put in their home life—unselfishness, cleanliness, and kindness. The world needs it. I don't suppose the world as a whole was ever more in need of kindness than it is now.

We need not ask ourselves why the world needs help. You have got to cast your mind over the world and you will get the answer. Europe partly devastated and still hating. Russia starving; Capital and Labour, like nations, almost as far apart as ever before. I suppose this must be the aftermath of war. You can't let Hell loose on earth for four years, and expect to find Paradise at the end.

---

[3] Before the Convention of the League of Women Voters, Baltimore.

Yet when I speak of war, I don't mean that it was all hell. There was one aspect of war which was better than anything I have found in the aftermath of war. There was a sort of kindliness and pulling together among all classes of the population, and one felt that at last a Brotherhood of Men was coming about. At least, that is how it was in England, and I feel certain that it must have been the same over here.

A common purpose shared by a whole nation, if that purpose is one of sacrifice, idealism, and helpfulness, is a wonderful thing. Think what a common purpose shared by many nations—a purpose with an ideal and helpfulness and a sacrifice of self—would be. This is what the war should have left—and even though, I admit, it is not obvious, I cannot help believing that that common purpose remains—remains anyhow in the hearts of those who suffered and in the hearts of those who care.

I cannot speak for the women of Europe, but I think I can speak for the women of England, and I say that they, through suffering, have determined that so far as within them lies, there is no sacrifice too great to make for the cause of peace. I have seen the women of England when they were determined. I have seen them tried and not found wanting. I can tell you it was a glorious sight. You may read diaries of the war which tell of dinner parties and plenty in London; but that no more represents the women of England than a night dancing-club in New York or a redlight district in some city here represents the women of America.

I will tell you what the spirit of English women was and is: The Bishop of Exeter, Lord Robert Cecil's brother, had two splendid boys killed in the first three years of the war. The last year of the war 2,000 American, Submarine Chaser sailors were stationed in Plymouth, which is in the Bishop's diocese. His wife, Lady Florence, did everything she could to make these American boys less lonely. She had as many as she could for Christmas, and hardly ever was her house without some of them. About January, 1918, just before one of the fiercest battles, she said to her sister: "I don't believe I could go on if Jack (her last son) was taken." The next morning a wire came saying Jack was killed. This was on a Monday. On Thursday, Lady Florence had planned an afternoon party for your sons—those gallant submarine chasers. When she arrived at Plymouth, and I saw her white, stricken face, I begged her not to have the boys—they would just remind her of Jack as he had been. She looked at me with eyes I can never forget and said: "But, Nancy, they too are far away from home, and we must do all we can." The party went off and the boys, never guessing her sorrow, were charmed as usual with the Bishop and his wife's cheerful kindness. That night I walked around to the American Y.M.C.A., and in talking to some of the boys told them of Lady Florence's sorrow. One boy, with tears in his eyes, broke out: "Oh, why did you let her do it?" Then he said: "If ever any one speaks ill to me of England, I don't feel that I could keep from killing them." That, friends, was the spirit of the women of England. Suffering only made them kinder and braver, and that's why I love and admire England.

Now, what can we do—the English speaking women of the world? And I cannot help feeling that we have got most all of the women with us—but what can we do to help the whole world on? We cannot live for ourselves alone and get peace. We cannot even get happiness, and I doubt whether we can get plenty. We must somehow rectify the mistakes of the stronger sex when left alone, and we must do it soon.

When America came into the war, Europe saw the dawn of a new hope— America in the war to end wars. When America went out of the peace Europe was dumbfounded. Idealism took America into the war; idealism did not take her out of the peace, no matter what politicians say.

The League of Nations was started by America, and by an American. Some seem to think only of the starter, and forget it was the high purpose of his people who gave the impetus which brought the League from America to Europe. When we go for a great ideal we go for the ideal and not for the idealist. It's a principle we should follow and not be side-tracked by a personality. Let us see what the League, even without America, Germany, and Russia, has done already. If we realise some of its achievements we may be inspired to give it greater trust, and add to its number of associated nations. The League of Nations, quite apart from its political work, has active humanitarian sections dealing with health, labour conditions, traffic in opium and drugs, and the White Slave Traffic. Each one of these must surely find hundreds of thousands of women backers in the United States. We want your help inside the League to bring on backward countries, whether it be to protect the world from war or from plagues, or to protect young girls from what is worse than plagues.

But I have not come here as a foreigner to tell any one—be it man, senator, or woman voter—what to do. You have invited me to an American Convention. You have not asked me because I am an English legislator. But you have invited me back to the land of my birth—to the Home of my father, from the Home of my forefathers, and, like the returned prodigal, you overwhelm me with love. Yes, it is true I have been in a far country. I believe I have been fighting there for the same ideals that Mrs. Catt has worked so successfully for here. I am deeply grateful that you should have asked me to come and discuss with you questions which interest all women.

As I understand it, you, in the League of Women Voters, are not creating a new party—a woman's party—to run sex candidates in opposition to the Democratic and Republican party candidates. Some people fear you want to do this. I am sure you are right not to do so. I did not stand for Parliament as a sex candidate. I represent a Division of Ply mouth—one of the most important naval ports of England. Thousands of my supporters are English sailors. But this does not prevent me fighting, and fighting hard, for questions where there is a woman's point of view—questions of morality, the protection of young girls.

Some men don't like it. But the best men—a growing number of men, I find—are supporting me.

You are right not to make a new political party. You are equally right to try to lift and raise and improve the platforms of both the big political parties by joining them. See that you send neither windbags nor carpetbaggers to represent you.

The big contribution you can make to politics and national life is to face and tackle the moral standard. Insist upon a single standard of morality—not by lowering our standard; but by raising the men's standard to that of women. Do that in America. We are working for it in England. If America and England do it, then all countries must follow. In some countries women are still looked upon too much as mere physical instead of mental companions. It is partly the fault of the women. They will always be that until they get a higher sense of companionship. The right-minded women want to be companions in the truest sense of the word, and the right-minded men want to have them so. It is easy enough to attract men; it is harder to help them. The single moral standard not only helps women, it helps men; *it helps nations.*

You cannot be material in your domestic life and be spiritual in your national life. You cannot be material in your national life and be idealistic in your international relations. Lust creates the spirit of War; it is incompatible with the spirit of Peace. The material man lives and dies. It is the spiritual man who never dies. So with nations. No material nations, however powerful, have ever survived.

The peace which the world wants is not the peace which comes from a smashing conquest—that sort of peace is apt to sow the seeds of vengeance. I believe the women can help to bring to the world the real peace the spiritual peace—the Peace which passeth all understanding.

Always remember St. Paul's words; they apply particularly to women: "God hath not given us the spirit of fear, but of power and of love and of a sound mind." We can only bring this spirit into world politics if we have got it in our hearts. Let us prove to all nations that we are not only talkers, but doers.

IV[4]

*"The most practical thing in the world is
common sense and common humanity."*

I DO not know who has been kinder to me since I got home, the public or the Press. I do know that if the Press had not been so kind the public would never have been. I knew that when I came home there would be some personal friends and relations who would be glad to see me, and then I knew there would be some people who, because of my political views, would be glad to see me. But I did not expect what I got. I did not expect this tidal wave of welcome. You have swept me off my feet.

When a person leaves his or her own country and goes to another, naturally there's apt to be a prejudice against them in both countries. I felt it myself. Then when that person—I can't say unfortunate person—happens to care deeply about both countries, and even more deeply about things concerning all countries, her task is not made easier. It's easy enough to take the easy way in any country. It's not always so easy to take what you feel is the right way in any country, but here I am—a proof to all countries that England and America will give you a chance if you can prove to either of them that what you are striving for is something which will hurt no man, woman, or child of any country, but which you earnestly feel is going to help all countries.

Now you will ask—What is this pearl of great price? What does this woman think will help all countries? I'll tell you what is the pearl of great price that I am striving for. I am striving to take into public life what any man gets from his mother and most men get from their wives if they chose wisely. The kind of thing you have had in your home life, the kind of thing that has made it possible for you to be here to-day is the unselfishness, the courage, and the vision and the clean love of your mother. That quality has done more than anything in the world to make up civilisation. Men know that and we women know it, too; and we feel that if we can get a little of that into public life, that is our only contribution. That is the only thing we have got. We are not

---

[4] Before the Associated Press, New York.

coming just as women. Women are of no more use than men. It is what we bring that is going to be useful, and a great many of us think that we have more moral courage sometimes than men. Women know that physical courage is easy enough but moral courage takes a bit of doing. We feel that we have got moral courage, and we know that we have got a clean love, and we know that we have got to be unselfish. If we were not unselfish you would not be here. That is the mothers' contribution to life. We are bound to be unselfish, and we think we have got a great vision. It is that which we ask you to accept. That is all we want to do. We don't want to go into politics because of ourselves.

We realize, as we realized when we raised you, that to make you perfect we have to do a great many disagreeable things; but we never flinched, and your mothers never flinched. They spanked you when you needed it, and they loved you when you needed it, and they sympathised with you when you needed it, but a really good mother never flinches from what is disagreeable, and we are not going to flinch now. We are ready to go into the political arena, and "arena" well describes it. There are many stout old Pagans prancing around in it still. However, we are willing to go in. We are willing to do our bit if you will let us help. Don't be frightened at us and don't discourage us too much. We know that your public life, just as much as your private life, needs this mothering thought. When you are blundering around, sometimes a woman sees as quick on public things as she does on private. You men think we women talk so much. It is true, we do; but even then we don't tell you half we know.

You'll be saying this sounds nice and uplifting, but we must get down to practical politics. What are practical politics? The politics that lead to war are not practical, and the same things that lead to bad politics lead to war. The most practical thing in the world is common sense and common humanity. It is the world's great need to-day. Leaving aside the vision of what a world needs, what we need is confidence, coöperation—and I would like to add another— conferences. I know it is not a popular word in America, but you need conferences. We have tried others and they have failed. Also, we have got to get to work. The world wants work. What's the most practical way to start work? Trade. Establish confidence—first, confidence between Capital and Labour, then confidence in your government, then confidence in other nations. The Washington Conference showed that coöperation and confidence were the watchwords of progress. The employer must realise that he's dealing with a human being, and the worker must realise that the employer has got some quality which he needs and lacks, otherwise the scales might be weighted the other way. These seem to be the essential facts which Capital and Labour should not forget. They were forgotten in Russia with dire results. The fault, though, began with the employer class in Russia. Don't let us forget that. Then after getting Capital and Labour together, we must get trade. The only solution for unemployment is employment—for the workless, is work. In the modern world no big nation can get work for all unless it trades with all. The best way to trade with all countries is to know all countries, and that's where the Press—you, gentlemen—come in. Bring out the best in all countries, get understanding, confidence, good-will. You cannot have international trade without international confidence. Russia proves this. Good-will is good business. It is for the Press to unite countries for trade and prosperity and peace.

Governments depend for their views of foreign countries, upon their ambassadors. Ambassadors get to know foreign governments. Foreign correspondents are unofficial ambassadors for the people. The Press can supplement official channels of communication by telling the people of each country not only about the governments but about the peoples. They can get the news and spread it quickly. They can get it to the man in the street. I know many of the American foreign correspondents. And I have heard frequently about the others. They are most able men, a credit to the American Press. They are trustworthy. That is the opinion formed by the people who know in England. I am glad to be able to repeat this opinion here to-day. If the Press wants to unite countries it can. If it wants to disunite them, it can. But the Press is just like a person in this. If someone tells you constantly of another's shortcomings and faults and extols his own virtues, you begin sooner or later to avoid that person. You feel, "Well, hang it all, he's not quite so bad as that anyhow. I don't like always hearing of people's failings. I like to hear what's nearest the truth about them and then I can judge whether I like them or not." So it is with the Press; if it gives us accurate, fair news, we can judge for ourselves whether it's white Press or yellow. We even see that people aren't so stupid as they look. Thinking people find out that facts based on prejudice cease to be facts. Mr. Davis told you all of this in a far better style and manner last year. The world has progressed a little since be spoke to you. We must be grateful even for this little. We must be deeply grateful for the Washington Conference.

I believe the whole world longs for peace. But we never get anything in this world and we certainly never get to heaven without striving for it.

America wants peace. America started the League of Nations. All Europe looks to America, not for large armies, not even for food, but for a great moral lead.

Lead us toward peace Help us! Help us! Don't just look on our faults—help us to be better! Gentlemen, if we know the better way—let us see to it that we take it.

Once more I beg of you to remember your power. If only your motto could be to unite the world, send no thought which would not bless or cheer, purify or heal—then we should, as the soldiers say, "get on with the peace."

V[5]

"I fear bombs in politics far less than I do apathy."

I AM here as a sort of dual personality. When I speak to the League of Women Voters, I am speaking as a woman interested in women the Whole world over. When I am asked to speak as a Member of Parliament to men and women, then I must speak with the full responsibility of a Member of Parliament, from the most up to-date and glorious constituency in England, namely, Plymouth.

It takes a good deal of prayer to keep me humble. To be born in Virginia and to represent Plymouth, is enough to turn a stronger head than mine. The Good Book tells us to love all men, also the greater the loving the greater the life. I am fortunate in loving two great countries, but their greatness will be tested by their attitude to lesser countries. To-day I am speaking as a woman and not as a Member of Parliament. The League of Women Voters, I realise, is not the only political league of women in America, but it has the merit of being non-party. I, as an outsider, could not come over and speak here as a party politician, but I come as a woman, speaking to non-party women, interested in something bigger than any party.

When entering Parliament nearly two years ago, I went as a party candidate, a Coalition Unionist. The Coalition was a combination of Unionists and Liberals and Labour, who wanted to coöperate and felt that Lloyd George was the best man to win the Peace, as he had done more than any single statesman to win the war. When I got into the House of Commons I realised that as for certain problems, such as moral questions which are of vital interest to women, no political party cared sufficiently or realised how much women cared. As a result, Liberal and Unionist and Labour men often put such questions in their programme, but more often they sat down when the time came to stand up and fight for them.

It is my honest and convinced belief that there are some questions vital and international, which women see with a more unclouded vision than men,

---

questions which only women will fight for. That is why I am so keen about helping women voters, not only in England and America, but in all countries. There are things bigger than parties, even bigger than countries, though neither party nor country likes to think that anything is bigger than itself.

If only we, the new-comers of political life, can keep that greater vision of bigger things before us, then the world will become more the sort of place one dreams of and less the kind of nightmare one dreams in.

Can we change it? Are we really different from men? I hope so. If we were like men, then there would be no use giving us the vote. It is because we are different that we hope to help, and yet women are like men in this. They vary! The women who attend prize-fights, the woman who keeps her husband's nose to the grind stone because of her personal demands and vulgar ambition to outshine and out-do her next-door neighbour, are just as hampering to real civilisation as the old-fashioned bar-room loafer, and more so. That old-fashioned bar-room bum was so obviously a warning to all—the ambitious, selfish wife or daughter is not so obvious; often she's for a time most attractive, yet the man whose soul is striving and who finds himself tied down to one of these women will tell one that their charm soon turns to dust and ashes. So when I speak of women I only mean real women, and real women are the women who care for real things. After all, it's only people who care about real things that have got us on as far as we are—not very far I'll admit—yet we are advancing. Crass materialism is going. The war of 1914 was just a war of ideals. Germany said might was right—we are mighty—we must expand—we must govern the world. The Kaiser with his God's help led a misguided and misdirected people up against the Democracies of the World, who, though they don't live up to their ideals, have at least got beyond believing in the Divine Right of Kings. King John of England found that out in 1214, and the Constitution of America was based on laws which men fought and died for in England long before they set sail for other lands. I am told that I have forgotten that Columbus discovered America. He discovered it, but some have forgotten that he didn't settle it. It's well to remember those first settlers. It's always well to remember unselfishness, courage, and determination, and people who gave up all for a high ideal. Now I don't come from Puritan stock; we in Virginia were almost comfortably settled before the Puritan Fathers set sail—and they meant to land in Virginia! Yet no one can look back on that gallant band of men and women without admiring and almost reverencing them. Those are the kind of people who make Civilisation, people who subordinate the material to the spiritual. They may be rare, but they are the light which shines in darkness. Throughout history Materialism has wrecked Civilisation. Now I maintain that women, just from their very natures, must have more vision than men. Why is it that you have just had a Mother's Day, not a Father's Day? Isn't it because of the subtle unnamable something about a mother which men and women feel? It's well for a nation to have a Mother's Day; it's well for those who celebrate this day to stop and think what kind of man or woman their mothers would like them to be. As a mother, I know that above all things, what we desire for our children is clean-mindedness and honesty. We know that if all our children had that, much of the old world's misery would dissolve and disappear.

Just take one thing which may seem small, but it's of vast importance. Do you believe that if women had been voting as long as men that we should have allowed almost the most important people in the country to be underpaid? I mean the teachers. Any woman who has children or who deals with other people's children realises what infinite patience, tact, love and long-suffering it takes to train and teach children properly. They also realise that they, the teachers and mothers of the nations, are forming the mind of the nation. And yet *all* nations have left teachers in a rut for years and years, and allowed them to toil for a mere pittance. If women had been voters and organised voters, this would never have happened!

I urge the League of Women Voters not to disband and go into parties yet awhile. Naturally, you must vote with parties, and later on you will very likely get tied up like men into parties, but I don't feel that the time is ripe. As women we must have organisation to educate ourselves, not on party lines, but on national lines. Raise the programme of all parties; that is what you are doing now. I beg you to keep on. The Democrats and Republicans will both try to catch you. Don't let them catch you napping. Don't become just fodder for political cannon. Form your programme and make all the parties adopt it. Begin in your home towns, begin at once. Get your politics straight. The only way to get cleaner and better politics is to come out and work. In Chicago, we hear just now of bombs. Well, I personally fear bombs in politics far less than I do apathy. If Chicago's citizens are thinking first and foremost of money-making, then the politicians who represent them will be true to type. If they think first and foremost of higher things, they will get better politicians. You and I get pretty much what we deserve in life, be it political or otherwise.

I believe Chicago has a great heart as well as a great head. I always mistrust people who make the most noise. Beware of men and women who are out for themselves. That's what keeps us all back—that awful self. Yet these people very often frighten politicians. I am told not to mention this or that subject in Chicago, especially the League of Nations. Now, if there is one city in America where one should talk of the League of Nations—surely it's Chicago. Look at your population. It's a City of Nations in itself. When you welcome other nationalities here, you want them to be good citizens. Do you believe that a man who forgets his mother is a good citizen? I don't. So it is with men if they forget their motherland. The war is nearly over—we never want another war. Some of us feel that if we could get a league of all nations together, we would go a long way toward preventing another war. And we are quite right in thinking it. The present League of Nations, even without America, Germany or Russia, has prevented three minor wars already, besides doing many other things. Just to-day we read in the *Chicago Tribune*—"League Draws Silesian Thorn Out of Europe." This brings to an end a dispute which nearly led to war between Germany, Poland, and other nations:

> Germany and Poland, through the good offices of the League of Nations, have ended their dispute over the rich Silesian coal and iron basin.
>
> They will sign a treaty of settlement providing for unified administration of the great industrial district by a mixed commission tomorrow afternoon in the presence of the council of the League of Nations.
>
> This is regarded as the greatest achievement of the League, with the possible exception of the international court project, for it brings to an end a dispute which nearly led to war between Germany and Poland, precipitated a local revolution, almost split the Allies asunder when Prime Minister Lloyd George and Premier Briand had their famous controversy and has held back Europe's industrial recovery materially because of the unsettled conditions it caused.

Do you mean to tell me that the Germans and Poles in Chicago don't want a league which will help their countries? I don't believe it. Don't forget also that the Irish, under the treaty recently made by Great Britain, can be represented in the League of Nations. But it can never be a real League until all nations are in.

So I appeal to all real citizens of my native country to urge upon this, the greatest federation of states the world has ever known, to cooperate with the greatest commonwealth of nations (the British Empire) which the world has ever known.

Let us give all less fortunate countries a chance. Let us be tender to all who suffer. Let our help go out to them in their need. The world needs the Anglo-Saxon ideals now. Don't be afraid of joining a league of peace. Be afraid *not* to join. The greater love is winning all the way down the line. The religions of the world are being judged by their fruits. The religion which makes men love all mankind; the religion where God is love, whose followers are loving, is the religion which will draw all men into it. Hate of any man or of any nation is a poison which kills. Women mistrust all who hate, all who preach or teach hate. In the name of God, who is Love, let us remember that by our fruits shall we be judged. Let us see that they are the fruits of the spirit, which are love, joy, peace, long suffering, and patience.

VI[6]

"Women are young at politics but they are old at suffering."

NOTHING I can put into words can ever make you Canadians realise what it means to me—a returned war veteran—to get back to Canada. I am a peculiar person, and yet I am a fortunate one. The Good Book says "the greater the love, the greater the life," and I have many loves. Being born a Virginian, I began by loving Virginia first. You Canadians should also love Virginia. She gave you some of your common laws, and Virginia led the way to America being governed by the best laws that any country has ever, so far, invented—the common laws of England. When people think—and voters should think—they will see that every citizen born and living on this great continent of America owes more than they know to the men who fought for freedom in England long before America was ever thought of at all. The British fought their first battle against autocracy in 1214. King John learnt then what the poor old Kaiser had to learn in 1918. Let the whole world remember that the men who first fought for modern democracy, fought at Runnymede.

There is nothing in being a Member of Parliament in any country; we politicians know that. But there is something very satisfactory in being the first woman to represent a constituency of the fighting men of Devon—my second love.

My third love is Canada. I do not love Canada for her hills or plains, or vast resources, or snowy peaks, or anything which you read of in guide books. I love Canada because of her fifty thousand men who gave their bodies as a loving sacrifice for their hills and plains and homes. The only thing worth loving is unselfishness. The only thing which mars life is selfishness. It was at Plymouth I first saw them land, your Canadian sons, and it was there that I realised that heroes away from home take a lot of watching.

I gave them all that I could, and how splendidly they accepted it. I found out there, during the war, that if you really love people you can say anything

---

you like to them—if you don't—you can't say "Bo" without somehow hurting them. I wish you Canadians could all have seen that realest bit of Canada in England—"Cliveden." We, my husband and I, only gave some of the buildings and the grounds and a few odd things. The Canadian Red Cross gave the rest, and I should like to say here in Ottawa that I saw a great deal of what all countries did for their soldiers, and no country did more than Canada. No hospitals were better equipped, no doctors more skilled, no nurses more devoted, and no men were braver. This may be forgotten in after-war grievances, but it should never be.

When I speak of what men stood from me, perhaps I had better give you some idea of what they bore with patience and fortitude. Many times a month I would give them a temperance lecture. Temperance lectures were needed—in war as well as peace. I would not begin with: "Thou shalt not." I began with a picture of Canada, their mothers, their sweethearts at home, what they wished and prayed for them. Then I would paint a picture of what having a "grand time" meant—drink, women, etc., and then the awful consequences which so often followed a "grand time"—sometimes prison, sometimes worse than prison, nearly always misery. They would listen because they knew I cared. I did care—and I still care. That's why I am in politics. One boy came up to me as he was going on leave, after one of my horrible talks, gave me his money and said: "Here, Mrs. Astor, you've just ruined my holiday." I might have ruined what he thought would be a good holiday, but I realised I had done what his mother wanted me to do.

I only did what hundreds of English women did for your sons. I never like speaking of war without speaking of what the women did. I know what Canadians who got the chance did no women ever did better. In England the whole nation had the chance and the whole nation took it. No, not the whole nation. Some wrote diaries. The people who wrote diaries in the War—well, they wrote diaries! Never judge the people of England by the people who wrote diaries!

But war is over; the men have gone; they can't come back. The question is—will their spirits go "marching on"? One looks round the world and wonders if they have died in vain. They did not die in vain; but they will unless we, with their unselfishness, go "marching on." America started the idea of a league of nations. Some persons for political purposes, started the idea that a league of nations would make American mothers send their sons across the sea to fight for unheard-of countries. All countries are alike in this—they all have a vast amount of ignorant voters and prejudiced politicians, always playing the political game. All countries have some apathetic people who are frightened of being drawn into public life; but let us thank God that all countries have some people of high ideals, true patriotism and sound sense—people who, having adopted the religion of Christ in its various forms, remember the Tenth Chapter of St. Luke, and feel they can't pass on as the Priest and Levite did, for they feel that those that lie stripped and wounded are their concern. Those are the people who will save Christian civilisation as we know it, not the civilisation we see, but as it might be. Even as it is, it is far better than any civilisation so far tried. You may say that this is idealism. Well, we have tried materialism and it has very nearly wrecked civilization; another time it will— so it ought. Civilisation based on materialism has been wiped out before, and pray God it always will be. So don't let us be afraid of trying more idealism. I have spoken to many thousands of people in America. I can't pretend to know all the problems of America; they are enormous. I only pretend to know a little, and that little is more than some politicians know, but they will know when it is too late. Now when politicians lack a great principle to fight for they have to fall back on something that will stir the popular imagination. In a country with a mixed population that is easy enough—there are some politicians in America who would be willing to win on any anti-British policy. Some people in America would try to misrepresent the League of Nations as a league started in England by England, for the benefit of the British Empire; they know perfectly well that it is not true, and politicians, like people, who are not telling the truth, are playing a losing game. I don't say that they will lose at once, but lose they will. All politicians and all nations who appeal to prejudice, hate, and self-preservation, which is only a form of selfishness, have missed the new spirit, the spirit of hundreds of thousands of men whose souls go "marching on." They are not so far away as some would think. These men belong to all countries, enemy as well as Allies. In the hearts of mothers of all countries the seeds of peace are sown. They are dumb as yet in some countries, they are apathetic in others, but, mark me, they are there.

Women are young at politics, but they are old at suffering; soon they will learn that through politics they can prevent some kinds of suffering. They will face the political issue as they have faced all others when called upon; few men have tried their mothers and found them wanting, and nearly all men have tried their mothers at some time. If women will only do their own thinking and base that thinking on Christ's teaching, I feel that our entry into politics will be worth while. We are the mothers of nations. If we individually judge our neighbours by their best and not their worst, the nation will do the same.

Canada has a great future; Canada more than any country can prove to America that the British Empire is based on laws which strive to be fair to all men and women, and do harm to none. Canada, with her French and English living in peace and legislating together can show that the Entente need never go. And Canada, too, can help me to explain to England that those who bark the loudest in America are those who least understand the best and most real in America, and very often are not Americans at all. All nations can have great futures, but all greatness can only be founded on what is truly great. Your fifty thousand Canadians have shown the way; let us never forget that the greatest Way-shower of all came teaching us to do unto others as we would they should do unto us. The nations that do that will conquer all opposition, surmount all obstacles and secure the only true greatness.

VII[7]

"Law, humanity, and Christianity make a perfect state."

EDUCATION is a dangerous thing unless it is started on the right lines. To start educating yourself for yourself is certainly one of the most misleading or mistaken forms of self-improvement. Real education should educate us out of self into something far finer—into a selflessness which links us with all humanity. Political education should do the same. The more I see of life the more I see that the only way is the narrow way and broad view.

When I landed here in New York about six weeks ago I expected to make two speeches and then go to Virginia and renew my youth. I have made altogether forty speeches—I spent only eleven days in Virginia and my youth has obviously not been renewed. However, in spite of talking, I have learned a lot—I have found out what a glorious thing it is to be long to two countries and try to be prejudiced against none. I've learned, too, how well all countries and all states think of Virginia, and well they might. It was in Virginia that the first laws of the best law-makers in the world were put into practice on this North American Continent—the common laws of England. It's a wonderful tribute to these laws when one thinks of how well they have worked away from the little island on which they were started. Changed and improved, if you will, but always the same. Here we see all kinds of people from all kinds of countries, living uncommonly well and peacefully under these common laws. They seem almost like the Divine law in that they embrace all sorts and conditions of men.

The great merit of these common laws is this: They enable everyone to work out his own salvation in his own way. Now, we know that neither the law nor the state can make a man. But a good law, and a good state can go a long way toward helping a man to make himself. We must have law, humanity, and Christianity to make a perfect state. I think we—and to-night I speak as a Virginian, not a British M.P. (so bear with me, as my time is

---

[7] New York farewell.

growing short and I won't speak as a Virginian again for some time)—we can feel that we have built this country on these three—a good deal of law, some humanity, and some Christianity.

Think of what America has taken on to her shores in the last hundred years! Now, it was not only humanity or Christianity which made us welcome the immigrants, any more than it was the search of these two qualities which brought them. They have come from necessity and we welcomed them from necessity. They brought much to the country and some have taken much away. It's amazing to see how many returned to their native countries after a period of about twenty-five years. In the meantime they have helped develop the country, and if your common law and common humanity and common Christianity has been brought into action, we will have helped to develop them, and when they leave these shores they will carry away more than mere money. When we look at Europe to-day we almost wish we had sent more.

Many of these immigrants make fine citizens. Just think what Mr. Straus has done for the infant welfare of this city. Many never leave the country again. But many of them until they learn better—just make a mass of illiterate voters who are used by our less fine citizens for political purposes, and their purposes are not for the betterment of our country or any other country, but too often for a richer and a fuller life in the worst sense of the word.

Now, I am getting down to political education—a thing of vital importance for every citizen of this country. This is a very interesting thing and something that we can be proud of. Both of our great parties, like most great parties in all countries, have their dark sides. It seems that all countries must go through periods of political corruption. Some countries linger in that state longer than others. We have suffered constantly from politicians or political crooks, but we have so managed that no party has ever dared nominate or bring forward any man but an honest man as President—they haven't all been Sir Galahads, or George Washingtons, or Abraham Lincolns—but they have all been like Cæsar's wife—above suspicion. That we may recall with pride. That's what I point out, when I hear people fearing that certain of our less desirable citizens will get high office. They just don't.

People are so apt to feel apathetic or indifferent about local politics. So long as the taxes don't go too high and the local "bosses" don't get too rich too quick—we shrug our shoulders and go on. I don't blame the local bosses....

This is an extraordinarily interesting age. But between spiritualists who see what the dead think and the psychoanalysts who see what we don't think, one has to be up and doing. So it is in everything—in religion, in business, in games, and in politics. If we are content to have only our Presidents fine and to have less fine local politicians, we are making it awfully hard for a President to do fine things. We are simply making it possible for less fine politicians to do anything they like. I don't pretend to be an educated woman, but I have a slight understanding of human nature and a positive nose for politics and politicians. Political education should begin with the A B C of politics. It should begin right down low, and for many of us it should begin right now. We have here one of the greatest countries in the world—it's a country which differs from any country in Europe, not only on account of its size and nature and natural resources, but because of its hopefulness.

Pandora never let loose a better angel thing than when she let loose the angel of hope. The three things that have struck me most about America are its hope, its spirit of confidence in the future, and its varied mysterious opportunities. It has an active and hard-working people, but added to this it has no outside cares, it has no great and powerful neighbours, and no anxiety as to what they are going to do. You have no idea what an obsession these things are in Europe. In Europe the soil is limited and over-populated; nations have to depend upon their foreign trade to find employment and food for themselves. All the time they are consumed with fear lest they should be attacked and their bone taken from them.

France is naturally afraid of Germany; Germany of Russia; and England, though not afraid of her neighbours any more than America is, is perpetually anxious lest the whole of Europe should sink into chaos. Not only would this intensify unemployment and bad times, but think of the added misery of those already suffering people! In England we can almost hear the cries of the starving children of Europe. You here are far away from all this, and for that and your innumerable blessings be thankful. No one asks you to give up a single blessing, no one even envies you any of them, but one can say this—when you realize your blessings and know what Europe is, what will you do?

Will you—will we—be like the Priest and the Levite that pass by and say "That starving, bleeding man is no concern of mine—it's probably his own fault—until he gets up and makes an effort it's not my job to help him. It's a revolting sight and simply spoiled my day"?

The other way is the way of the Samaritan. We can help him up, clean him up, heal him up, and let him share some of our blessings. I have no doubt which is the right policy—which is in the end the most paying policy.

The other day I saw that the American Government asked the British Government to help protect her oil interests in Mesopotamia through the League of Nations. I am glad to say she did it. Soon after I saw that the Allies sent a note asking America to join them and inquire into atrocities against a Christian population. America refused. I ask you which is the more important in the end, oil concessions or bleeding humanity.

Now, I don't want to leave here having said anything to hurt any person or party. All persons and all parties have been much too kind to me. There's enough trouble in the world to make one dread adding an ounce to it. But I should like just to say before leaving that I think the politician who, because of lack of principle, feels that he must appeal to prejudices or hatred—class, national, or international—is playing a losing game. They have missed the new spirit, and I believe as firmly as I ever believed anything that there is a new spirit abroad. It may be that this World War has set us thinking. It may be that women are the leaven in the lump, but as certainly as the Kaiser found might was not right in 1918, the politicians or parties who think that they will win out on prejudice or anti-British or anti-German or anti-what you will propaganda are doomed to failure. They may not fail at once, but fail they will. A mind that hates is a mind that is sick, and a mind which boasts of itself is as a frog which puffeth itself up. Only the mind which is genuinely out to help all humanity is the kind of mind which deserves and will get the support of all the right kind of people.

Playing politics may be all right when there is nothing seriously wrong with the world. Just now the human race needs human beings and not boss politicians. Quacks are failing all the world over and fundamentals are winning, and the safe policy for politicians and nations is not to do others, but to do unto others as you would they should do unto you.

ENGLAND

VIII[8]

"A fool without fear is sometimes wiser than an angel with fear."

IT WAS very kind of the English Speaking Union and the League of Nations Union American Committee to have thought of giving me this welcome. It was particularly appropriate that they should have asked the First Lord of the Admiralty to preside, and gracious of him to come. You see, if I have done any good in any way in public life, it's due to the men and women of England's most famous port—Plymouth. I think we can safely call it the most historical port in the world for two reasons: first, it was off Plymouth that the Armada was defeated. That may seem just a big sea-fight of ancient days. It was not thought so by the enemy at the time. They knew what it meant. It meant that England would be free to worship God in her own way—not free enough for some, but far freer than any other place in the world at that time. Then, from Plymouth, those who found their more advanced ideas about religious freedom hampered, sailed away to America, where they carried on their English traditions of freedom. There, in course of time, all men from all countries found freedom to worship God in their own way. I think it would have shocked them had they realised that some whom they welcomed to their shores would preach hate in the name of God toward the country from which they came; yet that is what they have done, some of these people who went to America. They have not understood that true freedom can never come to a man or a nation that hates. I, personally, have never feared people who preach hate—never—and in 1918 I was proved right. The nation which hated most was most handsomely defeated. The people in America who preach hate will also some day be defeated, and I don't believe their days is far off.

I am an unregenerate Anglo-Saxon, not because I am a Virginian-born British M.P., not because I care so desperately for the British Empire or the

United States, but because I care for something even greater than these two great countries. I care for civilisation based on Christianity. I'll admit that I have not seen much of it yet, but I've seen glimpses of it, and I've seen thousands of men lay down their lives because it seemed the nearest right. It seemed nearer right than the belief that might is right. They had a vision, and that vision goes on. It's in many a heart, and it's the hope of the world. Other countries have visions, but no other countries in the world have fought and won so many battles for freedom as the English-speaking peoples. The Reformation, it is true, began in Germany, but it was in England that its spirit flourished. Anglo-Saxon ism stands to me for true freedom, spiritual progress, high moral ideals, and a great sense of service. It is based on the fatherhood of God and the brotherhood of man. I know we fail miserably to carry out our high ideals, but we have no illusions about our virtue when we do fail. We don't talk nonsense about the super man or our thwarted souls. We know every one of us well enough right from wrong. We have an ideal, and if we will only listen to our consciences we realise that the Kingdom of God is within us, and it's our failure, not God's, if this Kingdom seems so far away.

Now there must be people in all nations who feel like this, but I believe that there are more people in the English-speaking countries who have been taught this than in any other countries. They have been taught a progressive Christianity. They have been taught to think for themselves, and that is why I am so keen that these two great nations should not only go on thinking for themselves, but should think how to help all mankind. To be great for ourselves is the poorest sort of greatness. It is pitiful, because it is not great at all.

I now finish my sermon on Anglo Saxon idealism, and turn to facts as I have found them in America. I am not here to speak of England; I did that for one month in America. Tonight I am here to speak of America, and I can do so with as much pride and confidence as to her greatness as I spoke of England's in America. Let no one mistake America's greatness—her greatness of heart. That's what struck me most forcibly from the first time I spoke there. You may not realise that my first speeches in America were on the need of America's coming into a league of peace. I spoke frankly and tried to point out why she was needed—that it was just because of the entanglements of Europe and her own happy fate and freedom from these entanglements that she, above all other nations, had such a chance to help on the peace of the world. No one desires to get any one else into entanglements, but we long to disentangle the entangled. If America had been able to stay in on the reparation question, with no axe of her own to grind, we all feel that the world might have been in a better position now—international markets might have been more prosperous and fewer children might have been starving. We can't blame any country for thanking God that she is not entangled in the European chaos, but we must count on the wise people of all countries to help to put the tangle straight.

Everywhere I went in America I spoke of the League of Nations. Everywhere I found hundreds and thousands of people eager to help along a league of peace. Much in this league of nations has been misunderstood and misrepresented in America. The Covenant became mixed up with party politics at election time. Millions of Americans seemed to favour some modified league of peace. I am sure this country has never considered the League perfect or above amendment; and I believe that changes could be made which would improve the efficiency of the League and which would at the same time make international coöperation acceptable in America. I may be wrong, I do not think so. Many in America have been frightened by certain clauses. They fear they might be drawn into European wars—as though England with her nine hundred thousand dead would ever join any league except to avoid wars. If certain clauses are unacceptable to America, let us change those clauses. No league can succeed unless it is based on mutual trust.

In America I tried to make them see that it was neither their money nor their sons, but their great moral support which was needed. I think myself that they realise it, thousands of them. The foreign-born American can hardly fail to see that the best way to help the country he has left is to vote for a real league of nations, which will include all nations. The League of Women Voters, which represents millions of women, is overwhelmingly in favour of some league of peace. Women of all countries want peace because we pay so heavily in war. There are women of all countries in America, and I feel sure they will work toward peace. They may give a lead to the men. They can if they will, and I feel that they will. America is bound to have a foreign policy if she has a Mercantile Marine! The thinking men and women realise that, and it's only the thinkers in any country that count. They are thinking hard in America, thinking so hard that they are playing havoc with the old Party machines. They are bound to be broken unless they represent the soul of the country. I don't believe that America cares more for oil concessions than for bleeding humanity. Certain interests may, but they exist in all countries.

If the Press of the country is any indication of the thought of the country, then we can rejoice when we read the American Press. Not the Personal Press. The Personal Press in all countries is very much alike and very misleading—in fact, it is a curse to any country. It's no good the reporters taking this down for most of their employers won't publish it. One reads the Press for news, true news and facts, not to have the news tainted by the personal prejudices of the owner. Unfortunately some newspaper owners don't realise this, but we, who read their papers, can only pity them and pray for better times. Now the Associated Press of America is a shining light in the country, because it tries to put true European news before the people. Mr. Melville Stone, and the gentlemen who helped him to build up the Associated Press deserve, and some day will get, the gratitude of the world. True international news is what we need to know to-day. I was much struck with the good European news that once got in the American Press. Over here, except for a few commendable exceptions, one would almost think that America was made up of bootleggers, drunken society girls, and cinema scandals. If that were true, it would be far better that America should never come into a league of nations. But that kind of news does not represent the country it is only true of those people who add to no country's greatness, and unfortunately are to be found in all countries.

I could talk to you for hours of my travels, and the wonderful kindness shown me wherever we went. It was so unexpected. I never started on a mission; I never knew that America would be so interested in what England had done and was trying to do. They warned me not to speak of the League of Nations, but I found that a fool without fear is sometimes wiser than an angel with fear. I had to speak of what was in my heart. No one could have lived through these last seven years and not had their hearts either broken, hardened, or just made larger. I tried to tell them about English sailors and soldiers, and above all English women. Many could have done it better, but I feel that England's greatness lies, perhaps, in her reticence. No English-born M.P. could have spoken out so. I had an unique opportunity, and sometimes when I feared I should fail, I remembered my friends in Flanders fields, and that gave me courage. However, it doesn't take great courage to speak out what you feel is the truth to people, particularly if they are your own people. It's a wonderful thing to belong to two great countries, but it's even more wonderful to feel that the hearts and desires of these two countries are striving for what is best and what is right. It may take time before America comes into her own, but her own is clear to me. She cannot live up to her high ideals if she tries to live to herself alone. I don't believe she wants to do it. She proved it at the Washington Conference. She had the chance to build the greatest navy in the world. She gave it up with as much grace as the greatest navy in the world gave up her long reign of the seas. There they showed the rest of the world how great they were. Sometime, somehow, America will confer again, and that will be to help the whole world, as England is so bravely trying to do almost alone now—to show men that her foundations are built on peace on earth and good-will toward all men.

IX[9]

*"America is no more a mere country of business men than
England is a nation of shop-keepers."*

IT'S a wonderful thing to feel that you in Plymouth, who gave me my first chance of public service, should be here to-night to thank me for any small service I may have rendered. I know that there are some here who never wanted to give me the chance, some who fought against my getting the chance, but that makes it all the more splendid and generous of them to come to-night. I hope that they will realise that, whenever a really big chance comes, the Member from this glorious old town will strive to do what is right, without party prejudice or partial affection. That's what I tried to do in America. I never did half as well as I should have liked, but at least I did the best I knew how.

My American trip will always remain a mystery to me. A mystery and an inspiration. As you know, I never went out on a mission; I was not quite so egotistical as that. I went to speak to the League of Women Voters. They asked me, and I realised that, being Virginian born and a British M.P., I might be able to explain to them a little some of the outstanding characteristics of the British. I could stand before them as an emblem of British Justice. You all must know that a certain section of the Irish in America (and only a section— many of the Irish-Americans are among the best and most highly respected citizens) have made hatred of England not only a plank in their religious teachings, which is the greatest of *all* crimes (for it is a crime to teach hate in the name of God who is Love), but they have also made it a political issue. They are highly organised, and not a silent body by any means. They have grossly misrepresented England, but I think they have over-rated their powers. To hear them talk you would think that England was a monster of greed and injustice. Their propaganda is subtle, but it is not really convincing. I think it is killing itself. It is a poor thing to preach hatred and it is almost suicidal to nourish it. It is a losing doctrine and is bound to lose, if God is true and God

---

[9] Plymouth.

is love. I am not afraid of those who preach hate—be it class, national, or international, for I believe that hate is a blind force, and that the truth about everything finally works through, though it takes time. This to me is one of the fundamental facts of civilisation. We are slowly but surely progressing nearer and nearer reality.

However, that is not what I came here to talk about. I am here to try to tell you of my trip. In the first two speeches I made, I spoke of England—her high ideals and desire to help the whole world. I spoke of the common bond between America and Great Britain, that bond I believe to be a common purpose of Peace on earth and good-will toward all men. I reminded them of what a great part the British Navy had played in making what civilisation we have. I don't believe that any other country in the world but England or America, with the greatest navy in the world, would have used it always for purposes of peace. I'll admit that before America was settled the navy under Drake was not exactly a missionary society, and yet it did missionary work, and made it possible for English ideals to go forth and spread the whole world over. I told them with as much pride as though I, personally, had bidden godspeed to Francis Drake and seen that his powder was dry.

I should remind you that Drake is as much a part of Virginian history as of England's.

I spoke of the League of Nations, and how it could never be a real League without America, and that America's greatness would never be true unless she helped the whole world; in fact, I just spoke out. I would have understood had they said: "This woman talks too freely; we don't want to hear any more of what she has got to say." I would have understood that; but they didn't do that. After my first two speeches we got wires from all over America, from all kinds of associations and people asking us to speak—business men, Chambers of Commerce, colleges, etc.—that's the wonderful part of the whole thing. I dared speak of England and the League of Nations, and of the pity that America should not be in, and they still wanted to hear I have always felt that not only are America's laws Anglo-Saxon, but her ideals are Anglo-Saxon, and I have always felt, too, that until people from other countries brought better laws and higher ideals than my forefathers carried from this country, that those laws and those ideals would be accepted, and would govern and guide all those millions of people from other nations who came to America. For the sake of humanity, one would wish America to accept better laws and better ideals if she could find them. I don't think she has found them yet. She may have improved them, but the background and bedrock are the same. Virginia did improve them, and I was reminded in Canada that Nova Scotia got her laws from the Virginians, who had improved them to suit a young country, and from these laws a great nation is springing. Let no one forget America's greatness. She is very young compared to the Old World. She may seem precocious—young people generally are—but she cares about real things, and her heart is as big as her territory. Ask any one who goes there, and they nearly all tell the same story of generous hospitality and a great sense of friendliness. I, being American born of only stout Anglo-Saxon forefathers, would naturally always love the real America, but this time I loved her more than ever, for I saw that my thoughts about her were right, and I loved her for letting me speak of England—how she had suffered, how she fought, and how hopeless she was at ever speaking of herself. I told them that perhaps some of her greatness lay in her reticence. When you do right, you can afford to be reticent. It is only people who are doing wrong who need to be continually talking. I knew that though ten Englishmen were being killed in the war for every two overseas men, to read the papers one would have thought that only the overseas men were fighting. So much was it so, that the German-Americans tried to use it as a proof of England's selfishness. She saved her own men, they said, and sent the overseas men into the worst places. You and I and the men themselves know better. It was England's dauntless chivalry which made her give first place in her accounts of the battles to her gallant sons who came so far to help her.

Then I tried to tell them what English women did—how they bore it all; and just worked and smiled and helped their sons when they came from America. You here in Plymouth know all about that, for you did it so well. You bound many a Yankee with your West Country kindliness. They won't forget. I went back and reminded them that English Kings found out in 1214 at Runnymede what the Kaiser only discovered in 1918. I reminded them that long before they set sail to settle America, Englishmen were fighting for freedom. They let me say all this, and they listened and were very kind.

And so we travelled far and wide, the two Plymouth M.P.'s of the Upper and Lower Houses. The Member of the Upper House was a far greater success than the member of the Lower House. They were slightly prepared for my democratic outlook, but they were totally unprepared for his. Imagine their surprise when they found him more progressive and democratic than most of the people that they saw about them.

Before I leave America, I must tell you that my welcome in Virginia was best of all—Virginia, England's first child and my first home. All I can tell you here at Plymouth about Virginia is this: I got a Plymouth man a job in Virginia, and I saw him when I got back home and he said: "Lady Astor, you are right about Virginia. I didn't feel a bit away from Devon here. It's just like home." And so I feel about Plymouth. It, too, to me is just like home. There's the same sort of naturalness about Virginians as there is about Devonians. We both have fine traditions, and perhaps we are both a little slow. The rest of the countries may pick out many faults in us, but they can also pick out many pages of history that would not have been written without us.

We went from New York to Baltimore, Washington, Philadelphia, Virginia, then Chicago—a wonderful place—and everywhere we found a great spirit of hope. It really seems a land of hope. Then we went to Canada. Everyone in Canada was kind, from the Prime Minister down, and most of my friends were down. They appeared all along the railway on the train from Ottawa to Montreal. When I was trying to rest a bit I heard at a wayside station two familiar voices—"Hurry up and come out, Mrs. Astor, we've come a long way to see you." There they were—two of the Canadian soldiers from the Hospital at Cliveden. Virginia and Canada did give me a very personal kind of welcome; so much so that I can't really speak of it, but I told them I realised that in thanking me, they were just thanking all the women of England who had worked so hard for their sons.

Now I don't want you to think that we took this trip for any personal purpose; that wouldn't have been worth while, and yet it turned out to be for a purpose—a purpose far above anything so small as a personality—things we believed in, not what we had attained. But we saw we had a chance to speak the kind of things that would unite, and we took it; and I firmly believe that some day we shall see the British Empire and America not bound together by any treaty—they may never sign any agreement—that won't matter, but seeing things as they saw them at Washington. There are so many people in these two countries who are working for what is greater than all nations—

Civilisation based on Christianity. I know you may look around and say we have very little civilisation and even less Christianity; yet we have a nucleus, a leaven perhaps, and some day it will leaven the whole. You may rightly say bitter things about America not coming into the League of Nations—no more bitter things than I heard some Americans say. I can't pretend to say that America will come into this League of Nations. I am no prophet; but I would stake my very life that some day and some hour America will come into some sort of League of Peace not to protect herself, but to protect the peace of the world. I know that there are hundreds and thousands of men and women in America who are striving for what is best and right in civic, national, and international life. There are people in all countries with vision, and they keep the rest from perishing. America is no more a mere country of business men than England is a nation of shop-keepers. We do business and we keep shops, but we don't end there. That's only where we begin. The countries who taunt us with that find, when there's famine in the world, American business men and English shop-keepers are the first to help.

To-day is Independence Day in America. Little American children are burning their fingers with fire crackers. American orators are burning their audiences with oratory. They are speaking of America's great fight for Independence. Let us all remember that the American War of Independence was fought by British Americans against a German King and a reactionary Prime Minister for British ideals, and that a large part of the British nation sympathised with the rebels. The same old British fighting always for freedom! The great American of that day was a Virginian—George Washington. Some one described him as one of England's greatest sons. He was a Virginian with only British blood—I am just the other way around—a British M.P. with only Virginian blood. I am no leader, no general, and no states man, but I hope I am a fighter, especially when it's a fight for peace. Many of us believe that until the British Empire and America get together and lead the world in Peace— Peace will be a long time coming. We feel, too, that in fighting for understanding between these two countries we are fighting for something far greater than any one country—for a civilisation based on Christianity.

THE END